Overcoming Negativity And Improving Emotional Management Review.

Dr.Steven Stemshorn

Isbn:978-1-312-46631-9

Table of Contents

Introduction 4

    Purpose of the guide...4

    Understanding Negativity and Emotional Management.........7

Recognizing Negative Patterns 13

    Identifying Negative Thoughts and Emotions......................13

    Triggers and Patterns 19

    External triggers 20

    Internal triggers 21

    Self-Awareness and Mindfulness.........................22

    Mindfulness...25

Shifting Your Perspective 29

    Defeating Limiting Thoughts and Adopting Empowering Perspectives: Overcoming Negative Beliefs...........................29

    Techniques for Cognitive Restructuring................................32

    Cultivating Positive Thinking 35

Cultivating Emotional Resilience...........................38

    Knowledge of Emotional Resilience 38

    Creating a Network of Support 41

    Practicing Self-Care and Stress Management.......42

    Stress Management 45

Emotional Regulation Strategies............................47

    Identifying and Expressing Emotions 47

    Expressing Emotions 48

    Healthy Coping Mechanisms.................................50

Overcoming Obstacles 52

    Managing Obstacles and Failures 52

    Overcoming Self-Doubt and Fear........................... 53

    Seeking Professional Help if Needed 55

Conclusion.. 56

INTRODUCTION

Purpose of the guide
The Guide's Objectives

This helpful guide's objective is to give you important tips, tricks, and strategies for overcoming negativity and improving your emotional management. People frequently experience negative emotions like stress, anxiety, sadness, and frustration in today's fast-paced and demanding world. These feelings have a big effect on our relationships, relationships with others, and general quality of life. But with the right information and tools, we can learn to overcome these obstacles more skillfully and develop a cheerful, resilient mindset.

This manual's main goal is to give you the tools you need to take charge of your emotional health. It aims to assist you in identifying harmful patterns, changing your viewpoint, and gaining emotional fortitude. You can actively work to replace negative thoughts with positive ones and radically alter your perspective on life by developing a deeper understanding of your thoughts and emotions.

This manual will also help you develop emotional regulation techniques. It will give you useful tips on how to recognize and manage your emotions. You will gain knowledge of a variety of coping skills that can effectively help you deal with strong emotions, including deep breathing exercises, mindfulness techniques, and journaling. By mastering these techniques, you will be better able to deal with difficult circumstances and keep your emotions in check.

This manual also stresses the significance of forming wholesome habits. It motivates you to make sensible plans, establish a wholesome routine, and incorporate acts of gratitude and mindfulness into your daily routine. You can lay the groundwork for long-term emotional well-being and personal development by encouraging positive habits.

The development of wholesome relationships is another crucial topic covered in this guide. Our emotional health is greatly influenced by our relationships with other people. We discuss the significance of cultivating a positive social circle, mastering the art of effective communication, and using conflict resolution techniques. By fostering healthy relationships, you can build a network of allies who will lift you up and support you as you work toward emotional well-being.

Additionally, this manual recognizes that challenges and failures are inescapable aspects of life. It gives you the tools you need to effectively deal with self-doubt, fear, and setbacks. It emphasizes the value of resilience and offers advice on when to seek out professional assistance. With the help of this manual, you should be able to overcome obstacles and come out the other side stronger and more resilient.

This manual's main goal is to give you a thorough road map for overcoming negativity and improving your emotional management. You can alter your mindset, develop emotional resilience, and live a more fulfilling and balanced life by putting the strategies and techniques mentioned above into practice. To achieve lasting positive change, keep in mind that this guide is only a starting point and that your dedication, perseverance, and willingness to put these techniques into practice are crucial. So let's start this journey together and realize all of your potential for emotional health.

This manual's practical and doable design gives you step-by-step instructions for putting the strategies into practice in your everyday life. It empowers you to actively participate in your emotional health and gives you the resources and tools necessary to implement long-lasting changes.

Increasing self-awareness is one of this guide's main goals. It emphasizes how crucial it is to be aware of your thoughts, feelings, and triggers. You can gain insights into the underlying causes of negativity and learn to address them effectively by cultivating a deep awareness of your inner world. This manual provides a variety of techniques and exercises to promote self-awareness, including self-reflection exercises, mindfulness techniques, and reflective journaling.

Promoting self-compassion is one of this guide's primary goals. Many people who struggle with negativity and emotional control frequently fall into the self-judgment and self-critique trap. This manual exhorts you to develop self-compassion, which entails treating yourself with consideration, tolerance, and acceptance. It offers suggestions for combating unfavorable self-talk, engaging in self-care, and accepting self-compassion as a potent instrument for emotional growth and healing.

This manual also aims to give you the tools you need to create better coping strategies. It acknowledges that everyone experiences challenges and challenging emotions from time to time. However, the key factor in how these emotions affect us is how we react to them. This manual introduces you to constructive coping strategies like exercising, reaching out for help from others, learning relaxation techniques, and finding creative outlets. You can effectively control and process your emotions by using these techniques, which will keep them from overwhelming you.

This manual also recognizes the connection between the mind and the body. It acknowledges the influence of lifestyle elements like diet, exercise, and sleep on emotional wellbeing. In addition to offering helpful advice for incorporating self-care practices into your daily routine, it offers insights into the significance of maintaining a healthy lifestyle. Making physical health a top priority will help you lay a strong foundation for emotional resilience.

The last goal of this guide is to encourage and motivate you to act. It acts as a road map for transformation and personal growth. It motivates you to dedicate yourself to the process of overcoming negativity and improving your emotional regulation. It emphasizes that change is possible and that you can lead a happy and fulfilling life if you put forth consistent effort.

In conclusion, this guide's goal is to give you a thorough and useful strategy for overcoming negativity and improving your emotional management. It aims to give you the tools you need to improve your self-awareness, emotional resiliency, and coping skills. You can start a transformative journey toward emotional well-being and lead a more satisfying and balanced life by putting the strategies and techniques described in this guide into practice. Always keep in mind that change starts with a decision to act, and that this guide is there to support and direct you along the way.

Understanding Negativity and Emotional Management

A Brief Overview of Negativity

The common experience of negativity has an impact on our feelings, thoughts, and general wellbeing. It describes a pessimistic or cynical outlook, a tendency to dwell on unpleasant experiences or results, and a focus on problems rather than solutions. Numerous factors, including individual experiences, cultural influences, and cognitive biases, can lead to negativity.

Negativity's Effect

Negativity in our lives can have a significant impact on our mental and emotional well-being. Increased stress, anxiety, and depression may result from it. Our capacity to think clearly, reason through choices, and uphold healthy relationships is also compromised by negativity. We become caught in a cycle of pessimism and self-defeating behavior that prevents us from breaking bad habits.

The Function of Emotional Control

The practice of identifying, comprehending, and successfully controlling our emotions is known as emotional management. It entails learning techniques and tactics to control our emotional reactions, foster emotional wellbeing, and foster positive experiences. The ability to control one's emotions is essential for overcoming negativity and enhancing overall mental health.

How Negativity and Emotional Control Are Related

Emotional control and negativity go hand in hand. Negative emotions that go unchecked can perpetuate a negative cycle and cause more emotional pain. Effective emotional management, on the other hand, can help people break this cycle by enabling them to deal with difficult emotions, reframe negative experiences, and develop a more optimistic outlook.

Recognizing the Fundamental Roots of Negativity

Understanding negativity's underlying causes is crucial for managing it successfully. In addition to past traumas, learned behaviors, cognitive biases, irrational expectations, or outside influences like the media or social pressures, these can vary from person to person. People can start addressing the root causes of negativity by recognizing the factors that are driving it.

Mindfulness and Self-Awareness

Understanding negativity and managing emotions depend heavily on self-awareness. It entails being aware of our attitudes, feelings, and patterns of behavior. People who practice self-awareness are better able to identify negative emotions when they happen, identify where they came from, and understand their own triggers and responses. Deep breathing exercises and other mindfulness techniques can greatly improve emotional control and increase self-awareness.

Overcoming False Beliefs

Negative attitudes are significantly fueled by negative beliefs and thought patterns. These ideas are frequently the result of distorted thought processes like catastrophizing, overgeneralizing, or personalization. Negative beliefs must be challenged by critically evaluating their truth, raising doubts about their veracity, and being replaced with more realistic and empowering ideas. Reframing and thought stopping are two cognitive restructuring techniques that can be helpful in this process.

Promoting Positive Thought

The key to controlling negativity and promoting emotional wellbeing is to think positively. It entails making a conscious decision to place your attention on the positive, cultivating optimism, and positively reinterpreting unpleasant experiences. Positive thinking can be developed through the use of affirmations, gratitude, and positive self-talk. Positivity can also be enhanced by partaking in joyful pursuits like hobbies or quality time with loved ones.

Negativity and Emotional Resilience

Emotional resilience is the capacity to adjust, recover, and flourish in the face of difficulty. Being emotionally resilient is essential for handling negativity well. It entails creating a solid support system, learning coping skills, and fostering self-care routines. People with emotional resilience are better able to deal with difficult situations, keep their emotions in check, and keep the negative aspects of life from taking over their lives.

Getting Expert Assistance

In some circumstances, a counselor's help may be need Seeking Professional Assistance. In some situations, a mental health professional may be needed for help managing negative emotions and thoughts. It's critical to understand when self-help techniques fall short and consulting a professional is required. A therapist or counselor can offer a secure and compassionate environment to explore more profound emotional issues, assist in locating the root causes of negativity, and offer direction and support in coming up with successful coping mechanisms.

Cognitive-behavioral therapy (CBT), dialectical behavior therapy (DBT), and mindfulness-based techniques are just a few of the therapeutic modalities that may be used during therapy sessions. These methods can assist people in developing more constructive thought processes and coping mechanisms, gaining a better understanding of their emotions, and managing negative emotions.

Learning to Control and Recognize Emotions

One of the key components of managing emotions is emotional awareness. It entails identifying and comprehending the entire spectrum of emotions that we experience. Negativity can be exacerbated by the tendency of many people to suppress or ignore unpleasant emotions. Being curious about and accepting of all of our emotions, even the difficult ones, is a necessary component of developing emotional awareness.

Emotional regulation comes after becoming conscious of our feelings. The ability to control and modulate our emotional responses in the right way is referred to as emotional regulation. Understanding the strength and duration of our emotional responses, identifying the situations and people that set off particular emotions, and putting effective control measures in place are all necessary for this. Deep breathing exercises, physical activity, mindfulness training, and social support are some methods for controlling emotions.

Self-compassion Training

In order to control negativity and foster emotional wellbeing, self-compassion is an essential skill. In particular during trying times, it entails treating ourselves with kindness, comprehension, and acceptance. In addition to giving us a supportive inner voice that promotes growth and resilience, self-compassion enables us to acknowledge our struggles without condemnation or self-criticism. Self-compassion can be developed through self-care practices, self-acceptance exercises, and awareness of our self-talk.

Fostering Harmonious Relationships

Our feelings and general wellbeing can be significantly impacted by the relationships we have with others. Negativity can be combated by surrounding ourselves with positive and encouraging people. Healthy relationships require clear communication, established boundaries, and the development of compassion and understanding. We can better navigate difficulties and deal with negativity when we have positive relationships that offer emotional support, validation, and encouragement.

Mindful Media Usage

Our perceptions and emotions are greatly influenced by the media we watch and listen to. Our mental health may be impacted by negative media, such as news reports that emphasize tragedy or conflict. Being selective with the information we expose ourselves to and aware of its potential emotional effects are both aspects of media consumption mindfulness. It is possible to control the negativity brought on by media influences by limiting exposure to negative media, looking for upbeat content, or participating in activities that encourage positive emotions.

Continuous Learning and Growth

Negativity and emotion control are ongoing processes that call for dedication and ongoing education. Recognizing that obstacles and challenges are a necessary component of the journey is crucial. Reframing negative experiences and upholding a positive outlook can be made easier by adopting a growth mindset, which involves viewing challenges as chances for learning and development.

Personal growth and the improvement of emotional management abilities can be facilitated by taking part in personal development activities such as reading self-help books, attending workshops or seminars, or looking for mentorship. Our ability to navigate life's ups and downs with resilience and emotional well-being improves as we invest more in self-awareness and the creation of coping mechanisms.

People can successfully manage their emotions and lessen the impact of negativity by avoiding negative beliefs and practicing emotional regulation. The process also requires developing a positive outlook, strengthening emotional fortitude, getting help when needed, and engaging in self-compassion exercises.

It's critical to keep in mind that controlling negative emotions and thoughts is a personal journey, and what works for one person may not necessarily work for another. It calls for endurance, perseverance, and a willingness to experiment with various methods and tactics. Additionally, it is crucial to look for expert assistance when necessary because mental health professionals can offer specialized direction and support.

RECOGNIZING NEGATIVE PATTERNS

Identifying Negative Thoughts and Emotions

It is crucial to develop the capacity to recognize negative thoughts and emotions on our journey to conquer negativity and improve our emotional management. Our well-being, relationships, and general quality of life can all be significantly impacted by negative thoughts and emotions. We have the ability to challenge these harmful patterns and opt for more uplifting and helpful viewpoints when we become aware of them. The process of identifying unfavorable thoughts and feelings will be covered in detail in this section, along with helpful advice and strategies to support you as you travel the road to personal development.

Comprehending unfavorable ideas

The inner monologues or stories that we construct in response to various circumstances, events, or experiences are known as negative thoughts. Self-criticism, self-doubt, pessimism, and an emphasis on potential issues or failures are frequently present. Negative thoughts can develop as a result of distorted thought patterns, prior traumas, low self-esteem, or outside influences. They can be automatic and subconscious, which makes it difficult to identify and deal with them.

Examining Unfavorable Feelings

The feelings we have in response to particular triggers or situations are known as negative emotions. These feelings can be anything from slight annoyance or sadness to strong rage or despair. Anger, fear, guilt, shame, jealousy, and sadness are examples of typical negative emotions. It's essential to comprehend and accept these feelings because they offer important insights into our needs, values, and areas in need of care and healing.

The Effect of Unfavorable Thoughts and Feelings

Our mental, emotional, and physical health can all be significantly impacted by negative thoughts and feelings. They may start a negative feedback loop that worsens stress, anxiety, depression, and even physical health issues. They may make it more difficult for us to build lasting bonds, work toward our objectives, and fully appreciate life. We are motivated to manage our negative thoughts and emotions by realizing the negative effects of doing so.

The Value of Self-Awareness

Self-awareness is a key component of recognizing unfavorable thoughts and feelings. It entails gaining a conscious understanding of our attitudes, feelings, and patterns of behavior. By developing self-awareness, we learn to pay attention to our inner experiences and gain understanding of how our thoughts and feelings affect how we perceive the outside world. Self-awareness is the cornerstone of personal development because it enables us to see destructive patterns and actively choose to change them.

Methods for Recognizing Negative Feelings and Thoughts Being present and paying attention

Being entirely present in the present moment while letting go of judgment is the practice of mindfulness. We can observe our thoughts and emotions as they come up by taking a mindful approach, which prevents us from getting sucked into them. Through non-reactive observation, we can spot problematic trends and learn more about our inner environment.

Try incorporating regular meditation or mindfulness exercises into your daily routine to help you develop mindfulness. These exercises can involve paying attention to your breathing, doing a body scan meditation, or just objectively observing your thoughts and feelings. Being mindful can eventually become a habitual state of being that improves your capacity to recognize unfavorable thoughts and feelings.

Journaling and Thought Records

A great way to reflect on oneself and gain understanding of our thoughts and emotions is through journaling. Every day, set aside time to write down your thoughts and emotions without editing. By keeping a journal, you can track negative thoughts that come up repeatedly and investigate the emotions and triggers that go along with them.

The practice of keeping a thought journal is another powerful method. Write down any negative thoughts you become aware of, along with the circumstances that brought them about, the emotions that went along with them, and any evidence that either confirms or refutes the thought. Negative thought patterns are challenged and reframed through this process.

Cognitive Errors

Common thought patterns called cognitive distortions play a part in unfavorable feelings and thoughts. Understanding these distortions will help you spot them when they happen and question their veracity. Typical cognitive distortions include the following:

a) All-or-Nothing Thinking: Viewing situations as either black and white or as having multiple shades of gray.

b) Overgeneralization: Making generalizations based on scant information or a single unfavorable experience.

c) Personalization: Believing that everything revolves around you or that you are to blame for all failures.

d) Catastrophizing: Exaggerating a situation's potential drawbacks and imagining the worst-case scenario.

e) Mind Reading: Assuming you know what other people are thinking or intending, and frequently assigning them malicious motives.

f) Emotional Reasoning: Believing that your emotions accurately represent reality and disbelieving logic or evidence.

By becoming familiar with these cognitive fallacies, you can recognize when you're engaging in them and challenge the veracity of your negative thoughts.

Getting Other People's Opinions

Sometimes we may not be fully conscious of our own unfavorable feelings and thoughts. Asking for advice from dependable friends, family members, or experts can yield insightful information. They can provide an unbiased viewpoint and aid in spotting patterns you might have missed. Be receptive to criticism that is constructive and seize the chance to develop personally.

Starting a Journal for Bad Thoughts and Emotions

Consider keeping a special journal to help you better recognize negative thoughts and feelings. This journal will act as a place for you to keep track of and analyze your unfavorable feelings and thoughts, enabling you to spot trends and make progress over time. Here's how to start a journal for unfavorable feelings and thoughts:

a) Designate a particular area or notebook as your journal. Make it simple to use and easily accessible.

b) To start, jot down any unfavorable feelings or thoughts that come to mind throughout the day. Be as specific as you can, mentioning the circumstances or triggers that brought them about.

c) Be sure to mention any accompanying feelings, physical sensations, cognitive distortions, or patterns.

d) Think back on each entry and consider contrasting viewpoints or opposing evidence to refute the unfavorable assumptions.

e) Regularly examine your journal to spot recurring themes, triggers, and advancements in controlling unfavorable thoughts and feelings.

The Value of Expert Advice

Finding and controlling unfavorable thoughts and feelings occasionally might call for expert help. A therapist, counselor, or psychologist can offer expert advice and support catered to your particular requirements. They can assist you in exploring the root causes of your thought patterns and helping you come up with practical methods for controlling your negative emotions and thoughts. Do not be afraid to ask for help from a professional if you feel overburdened or unable to move forward on your own.

Useful Advice for Recognizing Negative Thoughts and Feelings

Along with the methods mentioned above, the following helpful advice will aid you in recognizing unfavorable emotions and thoughts:

a) Engage in daily self-reflection: Set aside some time each day to think about your experiences, feelings, and thoughts. Examine any situations where negativity may have manifested itself, and consider the underlying causes.

b) Pay attention to your body: It often gives us clues about how we're feeling. Keep an eye out for any physical sensations that might point to the presence of negative thoughts or emotions, such as tightness, tension, or discomfort.

c) Pay attention to any repetitive behaviors, habits, or responses that might be linked to unfavorable thoughts and feelings.

Determine the circumstances or triggers that frequently result in negativity.

d) Live in the moment: Don't obsess over the past or worry unnecessarily about the future. To stop negative thoughts and emotions from spiraling out of control, practice remaining anchored in the here and now.

e) Surround yourself with positive influences: Develop connections with people who inspire and encourage you. Take part in activities that make you happy, inspired, and optimistic.

f) Use technology wisely: Pay attention to the material you consume on social media and other online resources. Instead of following or muting accounts that frequently arouse unfavorable feelings, look for uplifting and informative content.

g) Develop self-compassion: When unfavorable feelings and thoughts come up, treat yourself with kindness and compassion. Give yourself the same compassion and understanding you would extend to a friend going through a similar situation.

h) Take breaks and practice self-care: Give yourself permission to take frequent breaks to partake in activities that revitalize and restore your energy. Self-care activities can help you manage your stress and stop negative thoughts in their tracks.

i) Confront negative thoughts with evidence: Whenever a negative thought enters your mind, check to see if there is any evidence to support or refute it. Look for contrasting theories or viewpoints that might be more reasonable and well-balanced.

j) Have patience with the process: Recognizing and controlling unfavorable emotions and thoughts requires practice. As you proceed on this journey, be kind to yourself and acknowledge each small success.

Triggers and Patterns

It is crucial to examine the role of triggers and patterns on our path to overcoming negativity and improving our emotional management. Events, circumstances, or stimuli known as triggers cause emotional reactions in us that frequently result in negative thoughts and behaviors. On the other hand, patterns are recurring cycles of thoughts, emotions, and behaviors that we engage in and which frequently support negativity. We gain important insight and are better able to create strategies to effectively manage our emotions by comprehending and recognizing these triggers and patterns. In this chapter, we'll explore the idea of triggers and patterns, their effects on our emotional health, and strategies for breaking free of destructive cycles.

Triggers are defined as internal or external stimuli that cause people to react emotionally or behaviorally. They serve as triggers for a particular emotional or psychological response, which is frequently connected to prior events, assumptions, or learned behaviors. People's triggers can differ greatly from one another because what affects one person differently may not affect another. They may appear in various ways, such as as situations, events, people, thoughts, or sensory stimuli, and they may be subtle or overt.

External triggers are defined as stimuli that come from an individual's external environment. These may consist of particular settings, things, sounds, odors, or visual cues that cause an emotional or psychological reaction. For instance, returning to a traumatic situation's setting can trigger a person who has previously gone through it.

On the other hand, internal triggers come from within the person. They may be the result of feelings, memories, beliefs, or physiological experiences. These triggers could be connected to ingrained thought patterns, unfavorable self-talk, or subconscious associations that have developed over time. A person who has a fear of public speaking, for instance, might experience internal triggers like racing thoughts, an elevated heart rate, or anxiety before a public speaking engagement.

Because triggers have the ability to affect our thoughts, emotions, and behaviors, they are crucial for effective emotional management. By becoming conscious of our triggers, we can start to take back control over our actions and create plans to lessen their negative effects. It is important to remember that triggers are not inherently good or bad; rather, how they affect a person depends on their personal experiences and associations. People can learn more about their emotional reactions and work to develop better coping skills and emotional well-being by investigating triggers and how they relate to patterns.

External triggers

Are stimuli that come from the outside environment and may cause people to feel a certain way or start acting in a certain way. These triggers can take many different forms and be felt by the five senses. External triggers can be both good and bad, and how they affect a person depends on their individual experiences and associations among possible external triggers are:

1. Environmental triggers: These are components of the physical environment that have the power to affect feelings and actions. Examples include particular settings, such as a busy area or a serene area of nature, specific smells, such as the aroma of freshly baked cookies or the scent of a particular perfume, and visual stimuli, such as vibrant colors or an image that has special meaning to the individual.

2. Social triggers are those that happen as a result of interactions with other people or groups. Both verbal and nonverbal cues, such as voice inflection, facial expressions, body language, or even the presence of particular individuals who may set off particular emotional reactions, can be used in their analysis. For

instance, a person may experience stress or anxiety when around a demanding boss or joy and comfort when with close friends.

3. Situational Triggers: These triggers result from particular circumstances or situations. They can be things like situations, actions, or schedule adjustments that could cause emotional reactions. A job interview, a public speaking engagement, or a major life event like a wedding or a graduation ceremony, for instance, can act as situational triggers that elicit a range of emotions from excitement to nervousness or even sadness.

4. Media Triggers: In the digital era of today, media has a big impact on setting off emotional reactions. Advertisements, news articles, social media posts, and TV shows/movies can all act as external triggers. Media content, themes, and messages can all have an impact on how people feel, as can personal associations and prior experiences with particular media stimuli.

It is significant to note that an individual's emotional reaction or behavior is not determined by external triggers in and of themselves. Based on their particular perspectives, convictions, and prior experiences, each individual interprets and responds to triggers. People can learn to better manage their emotional responses and make the right behavioral choices by increasing their self-awareness and understanding the impact of external triggers.

Internal triggers

Are stimuli that come from a person's own thoughts, feelings, or bodily sensations and can activate emotional reactions or behavioral patterns. Because they are influenced by individual experiences, ideologies, and subconscious processes, these triggers are arbitrary and particular to each person. Internal triggers can come from a variety of things, including memories, fears, self-deprecating thoughts, anxiety, or physical pain or discomfort. Internal triggers are produced internally and have the potential to elicit strong emotional reactions, in contrast to external triggers, which are external events or circumstances. For one to effectively manage their emotions and develop emotional self-awareness, one must be able to recognize and understand internal triggers.

Self-Awareness and Mindfulness

Understanding and fostering a deeper understanding of oneself is known as "self-awareness."

Introduction

An essential component of personal development and wellbeing is self-awareness. It describes the capacity to recognize and comprehend one's own thoughts, feelings, and behaviors with an objective eye, as well as the effects they have on oneself and other people. Understanding one's strengths, weaknesses, values, beliefs, and motivations is a necessary step in developing self-awareness. People can make more informed decisions, develop their decision-making abilities, and create healthier relationships by cultivating self-awareness. This chapter will examine the meaning, elements, and methods of self-awareness development.

Self-Awareness: Definition and Elements

Self-awareness is made up of a number of elements that work together to help one understand themselves better. It entails reflection, self-examination, and introspection. People who are self-aware are aware of their emotions, qualities, flaws, values, and objectives. They are aware of their thoughts and behaviors and can discern how they affect both themselves and other people.

Self-Awareness Levels

There is a continuum of self-awareness, from low self-awareness to high self-awareness. People may only have a limited understanding of their emotions, motivations, and behaviors at the lower end of the spectrum. They might not be as aware of their advantages and disadvantages. People become more aware of their thoughts, emotions, and behaviors as their self-awareness grows. They gain a deeper comprehension of their values and principles, which enables them to better match their actions with their true selves.

Self-Reflection's Function in Increasing Self-Awareness

A potent tool for growing self-awareness is self-reflection. In order to gain awareness and understanding, it entails consciously examining one's thoughts, feelings, and experiences. People can recognize patterns, triggers, and recurrent themes in their lives through self-reflection. This method promotes reflection, which raises self-awareness. Effective techniques for encouraging self-reflection include journaling, meditation, and contemplative practices.

Strategies for Increasing Self-Awareness

1. Mindfulness: Mindfulness is the practice of bringing one's awareness to the present moment without passing judgment. People can observe their inner experiences without becoming engrossed in them by intentionally focusing on their thoughts, emotions, and physical sensations. By allowing for self-reflection and minimizing automatic responses, mindfulness fosters self-awareness.

2. Seeking Feedback: Getting feedback from reliable sources can give one important insights into their blind spots and areas for improvement. Positive criticism enables people to see their actions, attitudes, and effects on others from a new angle. It's critical to approach feedback with an open mind and a desire to improve.

3. Personality tests: Tests of personality, such as the Myers-Briggs Type Indicator (MBTI) or the Big Five personality traits, can offer a framework for comprehending a person's character traits,

preferences, and tendencies. These evaluations can reveal one's assets, flaws, and potential growth areas.

4. Emotional Intelligence: Acquiring emotional intelligence entails being able to identify and comprehend both one's own feelings as well as those of others. Self-awareness, self-regulation, empathy, and social skills are all components of emotional intelligence. People can improve their self-awareness and social interaction skills by developing their emotional intelligence.

5. Regular Self-Check-Ins: Making time specifically set aside for self-check-ins enables people to regularly evaluate their thoughts, emotions, and behaviors. It is possible to spot patterns, triggers, and areas for development by reflecting on daily interactions and experiences. It's helpful to reflect on the day by asking oneself, "What went well today? What might I have done otherwise.

The ability to be self-aware is essential in relationships. People can interact with others more effectively and empathically when they are aware of their feelings, thoughts, and behaviors. They are more capable of handling conflicts and are more aware of how their actions affect those around them. In addition, greater self-awareness fosters a stronger sense of authenticity, which encourages sincere interactions and more positive connections.

Additionally, self-awareness enhances personal wellbeing. It aids people in determining their areas of personal improvement. People can make decisions that are more in line with their authentic selves and lead to greater fulfillment and satisfaction by becoming aware of their values, passions, and purpose. Self-awareness also makes it easier for people to engage in self-care activities because they are more aware of their needs and boundaries, leading to more balanced and nurturing lifestyles.

Mindfulness

Developing Present-Moment Awareness for Inner Peace and Well-Being through Mindfulness

Introduction

It's simple to get sucked into the chaos and distractions of daily life in our fast-paced, technologically advanced world. We frequently multitask, make plans for the future, or dwell on the past, rarely pausing to fully experience and appreciate the present moment. The ancient practice of mindfulness provides a potent remedy for this contemporary conundrum. We will discuss the idea of mindfulness, its advantages, and useful tips for incorporating mindfulness into our daily lives in this article.

Describe mindfulness.

Being completely present, involved, and judgment-free in the here and now is mindfulness. It entails maintaining a kind and accepting attitude while paying close attention to our thoughts, emotions, physical sensations, and the surroundings. Mindfulness encourages us to ground ourselves in the present and experience each moment with curiosity and openness rather than letting the past or the future consume us.

Engaging in Mindfulness

1. Mindful Breathing: Concentrating on the breath is one of the basic mindfulness exercises. We can become more grounded in the present moment and develop a sense of calm and centeredness by setting aside a short amount of time each day to sit quietly and observe the sensation of the breath entering and leaving the body.

2. Body Scan: The body scan is a different technique in which we systematically pay attention to various body parts, beginning with our toes and working our way up to our head. This exercise

fosters a closer bond with our physical selves and increases our awareness of bodily sensations.

3. Mindful Eating: Mindful eating entails appreciating each bite of food while focusing on its flavor, aroma, and texture. We can cultivate a greater appreciation for the nourishment that food provides and create a healthier relationship with eating by eating mindfully and slowly.

4. Mindful Walking: Walking with awareness allows us to interact with both our surroundings and our bodies. A sense of grounding and appreciation for the straightforward act of walking can be attained by paying attention to the sensation of our feet touching the ground, the movement of our limbs, and the sounds and sights around us.

Gains from Mindfulness

1. Stress reduction: Mindfulness has been shown to lower stress levels by assisting us in objectively observing our thoughts and feelings. We can respond to stressors more skillfully and cultivate a greater sense of inner calm by learning to become non-reactively aware of our internal experiences.

2. Emotional Regulation: Consistent mindfulness practice improves emotional regulation by enhancing our capacity for emotion recognition and management. Greater emotional stability and resilience result from being able to observe our emotions as fleeting experiences without getting caught up in them through the practice of mindfulness.

3. Better Concentration and Focus: In a world full of distractions, practicing mindfulness can help us pay closer attention and concentrate. We become better able to focus on the tasks at hand by training our minds to remain anchored in the present, which boosts productivity and efficiency.

4. Improved Well-Being: Mindfulness has a significant positive influence on our general well-being. According to studies, it can lessen the signs of anxiety and depression, enhance the quality of sleep, foster self-compassion, and boost general life satisfaction.

How to Apply Mindfulness in Everyday Life

1. Start Small: As you get more comfortable, gradually increase the length of your regular, brief mindfulness sessions. Daily practice for even a short time can have a big impact.

2. Create Mindful Moments: Incorporate mindfulness into your day by making simple tasks like brushing your teeth, taking a shower, or brewing a cup of tea conscious. Pay close attention to your senses as you fully focus on the present moment.

3. Engage in Informal Mindfulness Practice: Pause periodically during the day.and focus your attention on the here and now. Use these moments, whether you're standing in line, traveling, or taking a break, to pay attention to your breath, the sensations in your body, or the surroundings. This unofficial routine will keep you grounded and lessen your propensity to go into automatic pilot.

4. Develop Mindfulness in Relationships: Engage in mindful speaking and listening when interacting with others. With no interruptions or preconceived notions, give the person you're speaking to your undivided attention. Communicate compassionately, paying close attention to the words and feelings of the other person.

5. Use Online Resources and Mindfulness Apps There are many online resources and mindfulness apps that provide guided meditation sessions, mindfulness exercises, and helpful advice. While you develop your mindfulness practice, these tools can offer structure and encouragement.

6. Attend a Mindfulness-Based Stress Reduction (MBSR) Class or Group: Think about enrolling in a mindfulness class or group. Your understanding of mindfulness can be strengthened and a nurturing environment for growth can be created by being a part of a group with similar interests and goals.

Overcoming Obstacles in the Practice of Mindfulness

1. Patience and persistence: Being mindful is a skill that takes time to develop. It's normal to run into obstacles and diversion along the way. Be kind to yourself and go into your practice with an open mind and without condemnation. Keep in mind that every moment offers a fresh start.

2. Handling Resistance: At first, mindfulness may meet with skepticism or resistance. Recognize these feelings and thoughts, but also remain open to learning more about the practice. Give yourself permission to accept the uncharted territory and experience any potential advantages firsthand.

3. Self-Compassion: Mindfulness entails developing an acceptance and self-compassionate mindset. Be kind and understanding to yourself, especially when you're having a hard time or your mind starts to wander. Throughout your mindfulness practice, be kind and patient with yourself.

Conclusion

A powerful method for cultivating present-moment awareness, lowering stress levels, and improving general wellbeing is mindfulness. We can establish a stronger connection with ourselves, others, and the environment by engaging in mindfulness practices. Be persistent in your practice, begin small, and incorporate mindfulness into your daily activities. Accept the opportunity that mindfulness can offer for development, self-discovery, and inner tranquility.

SHIFTING YOUR PERSPECTIVE

Defeating Limiting Thoughts and Adopting Empowering Perspectives: Overcoming Negative Beliefs

Introduction

Negative beliefs are deeply ingrained thought patterns that can have a big impact on our lives, affecting our relationships, self-esteem, and general well-being. These ideas are frequently the result of prior encounters, social conditioning, or insecurities. It is crucial to understand that these unfavorable beliefs are malleable and subject to change. We can challenge them and swap them out for more empowering and positive ones with awareness and practice. In this article, we'll look at a variety of tactics and strategies that can help you dispel false notions and live a more contented and assured life.

Knowledge of Negative Beliefs

Negative beliefs are the ideas and convictions we have about ourselves, other people, and the environment that prevent us from developing and being happy. These beliefs may appear in a variety of ways, including:

1. Self-limiting beliefs: These beliefs center on our alleged shortcomings or limitations and frequently cause insecurity and self-doubt. As an illustration, consider the statements "I'm not smart enough," "I'll never succeed," or "I don't deserve happiness."

2. Limiting assumptions or judgments about other people: These assumptions or judgments about other people may be based on stereotypes, biases, or earlier unpleasant experiences. They may make it harder for us to build lasting bonds and look after our relationships.

3. World-limiting assumptions: These assumptions center on a pessimistic or cynical view of the world, frequently producing feelings of hopelessness or a lack of faith in other people. Examples include "Nothing ever goes right for me," "People are inherently selfish," and "The world is a cruel place."

The Effects of Unfavorable Beliefs

Our lives are significantly impacted by our negative beliefs. They have an impact on our attitudes, feelings, actions, and even our physical health. Some typical results of unfavorable beliefs include:

1. Low self-esteem and self-worth: Negative beliefs frequently undermine our self-image and confidence, causing us to feel inadequate and self-conscious.

2. Anxiety and fear: Negative beliefs can keep us in a constant state of anxiety and fear, which keeps us from taking chances or pursuing our objectives.

3. Limited potential: Unfavorable beliefs act as self-imposed obstacles that prevent us from exploring new possibilities and realizing our full potential.

4. Relationship strain: When we hold unfavorable opinions of ourselves or others, it can be challenging to build deep emotional bonds of trust.

Fighting Negative Beliefs: Techniques and Strategies

1. Recognize negative beliefs: Acknowledging negative beliefs is the first step in challenging them. Pay attention to the negative thoughts that keep coming to mind to yourself. Analyze their causes and effects on your life by writing them down.

2. Challenge the validity of your unfavorable beliefs by scrutinizing the evidence that backs them. Negative beliefs

frequently stem from misconceptions, presumptions, or unreliable past experiences.

3. Seek alternative viewpoints: Look for perspectives or examples that conflict with your unfavorable assumptions. This can help you see things more broadly and give you proof to refute your negative thoughts.

4. Refute cognitive distortions: Cognitive distortions are thought patterns that support unfavorable beliefs. All-or-nothing thinking, overgeneralization, and emotional reasoning are examples of common distortions. To create more rational and realistic thought patterns, learn to recognize these distortions and reframe them.

5. Exercise self-compassion: Be kind and compassionate to yourself as you confront limiting beliefs. Accept the fact that everyone makes mistakes and has setbacks. Developing self-compassion enables you to accept your flaws and grow from them rather than beating yourself up.

6. Gather proof that supports your claims: Amass proof that backs up your empowering and uplifting claims about yourself. This can involve accolades from others, successes, or inner resources. Keep a journal or other record of these encouraging encounters, and consult it whenever unfavorable thoughts surface.

7. Put reframing into practice: Reframing entails consciously altering how you perceive and consider circumstances. Think about other, more uplifting explanations rather than accepting negative ones right away. For instance, if you receive constructive criticism, reframe it as an opportunity for development and improvement rather than taking it personally.

8. Disprove presumptions and biases: Unfavorable beliefs frequently result from presumptions or biases we have. Step back and consider whether these presumptions are true.

Encourage yourself to adopt a more unbiased and open perspective on people and situations so that you can learn and develop.

9. Surround yourself with positive people: Positive influences can help dispel erroneous notions. Find people who are encouraging and supportive of you and who have faith in your abilities. Take part in pastimes and endeavors that make you happy and improve your self-esteem.

10. Establish reasonable goals and acknowledge progress: Negative beliefs frequently result from a fear of failing or a belief that one is never good enough. Make achievable but challenging goals for yourself. Divide them up into more manageable goals and acknowledge your advancement along the way. Taking pride in your accomplishments can encourage positive thinking and dispel misconceptions.

Techniques for Cognitive Restructuring

Cognitive restructuring is a potent psychological technique that can assist people in changing their negative thought patterns and acquiring a more constructive and adaptable mindset. It entails questioning and altering negative or unhelpful thoughts, beliefs, and interpretations that contribute to emotional distress and negativity. We can actively restructure our thinking to better manage our emotions and feel better about ourselves in general. Here are some thorough methods for cognitive restructuring:

1. Spotting Negative Thoughts: Spotting automatic negative thoughts (ANTs) that appear in various circumstances.

  - Identifying thought patterns like overgeneralization, personalization, catastrophizing, and black-and-white thinking.

  - Being conscious of how negative thinking affects one's emotions and behavior.

2. Analyzing the Data:

- Questioning the veracity and accuracy of unfavorable ideas.

- Gathering evidence to support and refute these ideas.

- Examining alternative theories or viewpoints.

3. Cognitive Reframing: Reframing unfavorable thoughts by locating alternative, more reasonable points of view.

- Searching for opportunities or a bright side in difficult circumstances.

- Seeing setbacks as opportunities for growth and learning.

4. Rational Evaluation: Examining the logical justification for unfavorable thoughts.

- Recognizing cognitive biases and distortions, like confirmation bias and selective attention.

- Dispelling irrational beliefs and substituting more sensible and beneficial ones.

5. Decatastrophizing: Considering the probability and repercussions of feared outcomes.

- Examining more sensible and reasonable options.

- Understanding that imagining the worst case scenarios exaggerates the likely outcomes.

6. Cognitive Distancing: Stepping back and viewing thoughts from a more detached perspective.

- Treating thoughts as mental processes rather than unchanging realities.

- Understanding that one's thoughts do not constitute reality or define who they are as a person.

7. Thought Stopping: - Interrupting and substituting constructive or neutral thoughts for negative ones.

   - Stopping habitual negative thinking by visualizing it or by saying "stop" out loud.

   - Replacing negative thoughts with self-talk or affirmations.

8. Socratic Questioning: This involves challenging unfavorable thoughts in oneself by asking hard questions.

   - Promoting critical thinking and self-reflection.

   - Analyzing the data and taking into account alternative hypotheses.

9. Being thankful and having a positive outlook: This involves turning your focus to the good things in life.

   - Fostering gratitude for the good things in life.

   - Talking to oneself in a constructive manner and emphasizing one's accomplishments.

10. Practice and Persistence: Employing cognitive restructuring techniques consistently.

   - Exercise self-compassion and endurance during the procedure.

   - Seeking assistance, if necessary, from a therapist or counselor.

   - Understanding that everyone experiences negative thoughts and that these are a normal part of being human.

17. Seeking Support: - Attending therapy or counseling to get pointers and assistance with cognitive retraining.

   - Discussing struggles and experiences with dependable friends or peer support group

Cultivating Positive Thinking
Developing Positive Thoughts

Our general wellbeing and quality of life can be significantly impacted by the powerful mindset of positive thinking. It entails deliberately choosing to minimize negative thoughts and self-doubt while emphasizing the positive aspects of life, circumstances, and ourselves. We can build resiliency, enhance our capacity for problem-solving, and improve our emotional wellbeing by cultivating positive thinking. When cultivating positive thinking, keep the following points in mind:

1. Awareness: The first step in developing positive thinking is to become conscious of the influence of our thoughts on our feelings and actions. Pay attention to your inner dialogue and note any limiting or unfavorable thoughts that may come up. Being aware enables us to stop negative thought patterns and replace them with constructive ones.

2. Reframing: Reframing entails purposefully altering how we view and interpret circumstances. Try to find the positive aspects or the lessons to be learned from any experience rather than concentrating on the drawbacks or difficulties. Reframing enables us to find opportunities for growth and positivity by transforming our perspective from one of victimhood to one of empowerment.

3. Practice of gratitude: Gratitude is a potent tool for developing optimistic thinking. Spend some time every day thinking about and being thankful for the things you value in your life. By directing your attention to what is going well, this practice helps you feel abundant and content. You can record your gratitude in a journal, send thank-you notes, or just acknowledge it in your mind.

4. Positive Self-Talk: Pay attention to the internal dialogue you have with yourself. Affirmations and positive statements should

take the place of self-criticism and negative self-talk. Keep reminding yourself of your qualities, successes, and advancements. You can develop a resilient mindset and increase your self-confidence by engaging in constructive self-talk.

5. Surround Yourself with Positive People: The people and surroundings we choose to surround ourselves with have a significant impact on our attitudes and thoughts. Be in the company of uplifting, encouraging people who inspire you. Take part in enjoyable activities and expose yourself to inspiring media, such as books, podcasts, or motivational speeches.

6. Mindfulness and meditation: By teaching your mind to concentrate on the present moment without passing judgment, mindfulness and meditation can assist in developing a positive mindset. Being mindful enables you to be aware of your thoughts and feelings without getting sucked into them, which promotes peace and acceptance. Regular meditation can improve well-being, lessen stress, and heighten self-awareness.

7. Adopt an Optimistic Attitude: Make the decision to adopt an Optimistic Attitude. Optimism is the confidence that you can overcome obstacles, not the denial that there are difficulties or setbacks. Positivity results from adopting optimism because it enables you to approach situations with optimism, resiliency, and a proactive mindset.

8. Engage in Self-Care: Developing positive thinking requires that you look after your physical, mental, and emotional health. Take part in activities that will nourish and renew you, such as physical activity, enough sleep, a healthy diet, and hobbies you enjoy. Self-care is something you should put first if you want to be more positive and able to handle stress.

Positive thinking requires consistent practice and effort, but the benefits are worthwhile. You can transform your life, develop resilience, and overcome obstacles with grace and optimism by changing your mindset to one of positivity. Remember that choosing to think positively gives you the power to design a life that is more content and joyful.

9. Learn from Failures: Failures and setbacks are inevitable parts of life. Consider them as chances for development and learning rather than letting them dim your optimism. Adopt a growth mindset that views obstacles as temporary setbacks and has faith in your ability to overcome them by becoming more resilient. Consider the lessons you can learn from each failure, and use those insights to motivate your future efforts.

10. Work on your visualization skills. Visualization is an effective technique that involves imagining yourself achieving your objectives and enjoying successful outcomes. Spend some time each day picturing your success, happiness, and the life you want. You can train your mind to focus on the possibilities and strengthen your belief that you can achieve your goals by vividly imagining positive scenarios.

CULTIVATING EMOTIONAL RESILIENCE

Knowledge of Emotional Resilience

The capacity to adapt, cope with, and recover from the stresses, setbacks, and challenges of life is known as emotional resilience. It entails building a solid capacity for emotion control and regulation, upholding a positive outlook, and successfully navigating challenging situations. Emotional resilience is the ability to face adversity head-on while maintaining psychological well-being. It is not about avoiding or suppressing negative emotions.

1. The Nature of Emotional Resilience: Over time, emotional resilience can be learned and developed as a dynamic process.

   - It entails accepting the full spectrum of emotions, both good and bad, and realizing that they are a normal aspect of the human experience.

   - Being emotionally resilient does not entail being immune to difficult circumstances; rather, it concentrates on how people react to and move past them.

2. The Essential Elements of Emotional Resilience

   a. Emotional Intelligence:

   - Growing in self-awareness of emotions, including the ability to recognize and accurately label them.

   - Recognizing the patterns and triggers that affect emotional reactions.

   b. Emotional Regulation: - Creating effective methods for controlling and regulating strong emotions.

   - Developing effective coping skills to deal with difficult emotions like stress and anxiety.

- Acquiring skills to support emotional balance, such as deep breathing, meditation, or mindfulness.

Cultivating cognitive flexibility will help you adjust your perspective to changing circumstances.

- Reframing negative or self-defeating thoughts in a more constructive or realistic manner.

- Adopting a growth mindset, which sees failures as chances for learning and development.

d. Social Support: Establishing and maintaining solid relationships with people who are encouraging.

- Consulting dependable friends, family members, or experts for support, advice, and direction when facing difficulties.

- Developing wholesome relationships that are supportive of emotional well-being.

Prioritizing self-care activities that promote physical, mental, and emotional well-being is what is meant by "self-care" in this section.

- Making time for leisure pursuits, hobbies, physical activity, and other satisfying pursuits.

- Creating boundaries and engaging in self-compassion exercises to avoid burnout and keep resilience.

3. The advantages of emotional resilience include: - An improved capacity to deal with pressure, adversity, and uncertainty.

- An improvement in emotional health that raises happiness and life satisfaction levels.

- Improved productivity and motivation in both the personal and professional spheres.

- Improved ability to solve problems and make decisions in difficult circumstances.

- Improved communication and relationship skills, fostering stronger bonds with others.

4. Developing Emotional Resilience: - Having a growth mindset and accepting setbacks as chances for improvement.

- Looking for resources to learn emotional regulation strategies, such as books, classes, or therapy.

- Consistently reflecting on oneself and using mindfulness techniques to heighten self-awareness.

- Establishing a solid network of support and keeping the lines of communication with loved ones open.

- Taking care of one's physical health by engaging in regular exercise, eating well, and getting enough sleep.

5. The Function of Professional Assistance: - In some circumstances, consulting with mental health experts can be helpful.

- Tools and strategies tailored to a person's needs can be offered by therapists or counselors.

- Therapy can address underlying problems causing emotional problems and offer a nurturing environment for development.

It takes commitment and practice to comprehend and cultivate emotional resilience, which is a journey that never ends. People can strengthen their resilience and face life's challenges with more vigor and optimism by developing emotional awareness, effective emotion regulation, social support, and self-care priorities.

Creating a Network of Support

One of the most important aspects of our journey to overcome negativity and improve our emotional management is creating a supportive network. Our emotional health and resilience can be greatly impacted by those who support us, empathize with our struggles, and offer encouragement.

1. Understanding the Value of a Strong Support System - Recognizing the positive effects of a solid support network - Understanding the influence of social connections on mental health - Understanding the importance of empathy and validation

2. Selecting the Correct Individuals

   - Examining the traits you look for in a supportive person

   - Evaluating current connections and the degree of support they provide - Looking for communities and individuals with similar views

3. Maintaining Current Relationships

   - Speaking candidly and openly with close family members and friends.

   - Asking supportive people for advice, direction, and a listening ear - Thanking them for being in your life and expressing your appreciation for them

4. Increasing Your Network - Taking Part in Interest-Aligned Group Activities and Events - Joining Clubs, Organizations, or Support Groups Related to Your Struggles - Participating in Online Communities or Forums that Promote Growth and Positivity

5. Fostering Mutual Support - Showing active listening skills and providing assistance to those in need.

- Creating mutually beneficial connections based on respect and understanding - Supporting and empowering others on their own journey

6. Seeking Professional Support - Understanding when seeking professional assistance may be necessary - Seeking advice from therapists, counselors, or coaches

- Including expert assistance in your network for all-encompassing care

Setting Boundaries - Recognizing the significance of establishing sound boundaries

- Setting your well-being as a top priority by surrounding yourself with supportive people - Recognizing toxic or unsupportive relationships and taking steps to minimize their impact

8. Keeping in Touch and Sustaining Relationships - Communicating frequently and keeping the lines of communication open - Understanding that relationships require ongoing care and attention

9. Adopting virtual support - Using technology to connect with people who can be of assistance anywhere in the world - Taking part in online communities and support groups - Using virtual therapy or counseling services if necessary

10. Developing Self-Support - Understanding the value of self-compassion and self-care - Creating a strong sense of self-worth and confidence - Developing resilience to rely on yourself in difficult situations

Practicing Self-Care and Stress Management

Self-care is the act of doing things for oneself that are good for one's physical, mental, and emotional health. It entails making conscious choices to prioritize and care for oneself in recognition of the value of upholding a positive relationship with oneself.Self-care includes looking after one's physical health,emotional stability, psychological fortitude, and general self-awareness. It entails consciously carrying out actions that promote self-compassion, self-acceptance, and self-reflection.

Self-care activities include, for instance:

1. Physical self-care: Regular exercise, a healthy diet, sufficient sleep, good hygiene, and seeking medical attention when required.

2. Taking care of one's emotions includes: recognizing and acknowledging emotions, expressing emotions in healthy ways, participating in joyful activities, asking loved ones for emotional support, and practicing self-compassion and self-forgiveness.

3. Psychological self-care: Practicing mental health-promoting behaviors like mindfulness and meditation, participating in hobbies and interests, setting boundaries, controlling stress levels, and seeking professional assistance when necessary.

4. Social self-care: Maintaining wholesome relationships, spending quality time with loved ones, looking for social support, taking part in social activities, and establishing sound boundaries in relationships.

5. Spiritual self-care: Taking part in activities that are consistent with one's values and beliefs, such as showing gratitude, meditating or praying, getting outside, or seeking out a spiritual community.

6. Establishing clear boundaries is essential for self-care in both your personal and professional lives. Learn to say no to commitments or activities that deplete your energy or put your wellbeing at risk. Put your needs first and make sure you schedule time for rest, relaxation, and introspection.

7. Reflecting on oneself: Give yourself some time to think back on your experiences, feelings, and thoughts. This may entail keeping a journal, engaging in mindfulness exercises, or seeking therapy. You can learn more about yourself through self-reflection, spot opportunities for personal development, and make changes that are more in line with your values and objectives.

8. Taking part in joyful activities: Make a list of the things that make you happy and satisfied. It could be pastimes, creative endeavors, time spent outdoors, reading, music listening, or anything else that feeds your soul. Regularly include these activities in your routine.

9. Develop self-compassion by being kind, forgiving, and understanding of yourself. Recognize that you are only human and that everyone experiences difficulties or makes mistakes. During challenging times, be kind to yourself and practice self-compassion rather than self-criticism.

10. Making self-care rituals a priority: Establish a self-care schedule that includes exercises that encourage relaxation and wellbeing. This might entail taking leisurely baths, engaging in regular massages, practicing meditation or deep breathing exercises, or simply enjoying a quiet cup of tea or coffee in the morning. Making time specifically set aside for taking care of yourself is made easier by creating self-care rituals.

11. Cutting ties with technology: Take breaks from your screens and unplug from the never-ending stream of information. Take part in non-technological activities, such as taking a walk, enjoying nature,or having heartfelt face-to-face conversations with loved ones. Unplugging can foster a sense of presence and calm while assisting in stress management.

It's important to keep in mind that self-care is highly individualized, so what works for one person might not work for another. It's crucial to experiment with various self-care techniques and discover which ones speak to you personally. Regularly evaluate your self-care routines and tweak them as necessary to keep them promoting your general wellbeing.

Stress Management

The term "stress management" refers to the methods and tactics employed to successfully manage stress and lessen its detrimental effects on one's mental, emotional, and physical health. It entails identifying the telltale signs and symptoms of stress, comprehending its underlying causes, and putting healthy, adaptable measures in place to lessen its effects.

The main objective of stress management isn't necessarily to completely eradicate stress, but rather to improve one's capacity for coping with stress in a healthy and balanced manner. It aims to promote general wellness, strengthen coping skills, and increase resilience.

Depending on the person and their preferences, stress management techniques can vary, but frequently they include:

1. Self-awareness: Being able to identify stress triggers, comprehend one's own stress reactions, and spot early indications of stress.

2. Relaxation techniques: Taking part in activities like progressive muscle relaxation, deep breathing exercises, meditation, or yoga that encourage relaxation and ease tension.

3. Time management: Setting priorities, establishing attainable goals, and efficiently utilizing time to reduce feelings of stress and overwhelm.

4. Making healthy lifestyle decisions, such as following a balanced diet, exercising frequently, getting enough sleep, and abstaining from bad coping strategies like excessive alcohol or drug use.

5. Social support: Establishing and sustaining a strong network of family, friends, or support groups with whom one can discuss problems, get counsel, and find emotional support.

6. Problem-solving abilities: Developing efficient methods for addressing stressors and identifying workable solutions to lessen or eliminate them.

7. Boundaries and assertiveness: Establishing boundaries to safeguard personal time and energy and assertively expressing needs and concerns to lessen stress brought on by conflicts or a lot of work.

8. Stress-reducing activities: Taking part in leisurely pursuits, spending time in nature, listening to music, or focusing on the present moment.

9. Seeking professional assistance: When stress starts to significantly interfere with daily life or becomes overwhelming, seeking assistance from mental health professionals who can offer direction, therapy, or other suitable interventions.

10. Cognitive restructuring: recognizing negative thought patterns, challenging them, and replacing them with more optimistic and realistic viewpoints. This entails rephrasing unfavorable ideas, engaging in self-compassion, and cultivating a resilient mindset.

EMOTIONAL REGULATION STRATEGIES

Identifying and Expressing Emotions

1. Mindful Awareness: Invest some time in being mindfully aware of your thoughts, feelings, and physical sensations. Do this without passing judgment. Watch your emotional state for any alterations or shifts.

2. Emotional Vocabulary: Increase your understanding of a variety of emotions to broaden your emotional vocabulary. This can make it easier for you to identify and categorize particular emotions. For references, look up emotion diagrams or lists.

3. Body Awareness: Emotions frequently appear as bodily sensations. Pay attention to any physical cues, such as tightness in the muscles, stomach butterflies, or a rapid heartbeat. Link the corresponding emotions to these sensations.

4. Reflective Journaling: Keep a journal in which you can record your thoughts, feelings, and experiences. Review your entries frequently to spot any recurring emotional trajectories or triggers.

5. Creative Expression: Express your emotions visually or metaphorically by writing poetry, painting, or other creative endeavors. This may help you understand how you're feeling.

6. Non-Verbal Cues: Pay attention to your own and other people's non-verbal cues, such as their body language, tone of voice, or facial expressions. These cues can offer insightful hints regarding the underlying emotions being felt.

7. Take a moment to check in with yourself at various points during the day. Take stock of your feelings by asking yourself how you're feeling and writing them down. Self-awareness is improved by this practice.

8. Request Feedback: Reliable family members, close friends, or therapists can provide a second opinion on your feelings. Tell them about your experiences and seek their opinion on any possible emotions you may be feeling.

9. Mind-Body Connection: Pay attention to how various emotions affect your physical appearance. Consider how sadness may feel like heaviness or a lump in your throat, while anger may feel like heat or tension. This mind-body link can offer insightful hints about your emotions.

10. Consider Your Triggers: Make a list of the circumstances, experiences, or interactions that consistently cause you to feel strongly. Consider why these triggers affect you so much and the feelings they cause. This can make it easier for you to comprehend your emotional landscape.

Expressing Emotions

Emotional health and effective communication both depend on people being able to express their emotions. Here are some techniques to assist you in expressing your emotions in a positive and healthy way:

1. Identify and Describe Your Emotions: Give yourself some time to identify and comprehend the emotions you are feeling. When expressing your emotions, be specific by using phrases like "I feel frustrated," "I feel happy," or "I feel anxious." This step aids in your ability to understand how you're feeling.

2. Select the Appropriate Time and Location: Look for a suitable situation where you feel free to express your emotions. It might be a quiet setting or a private area where you can speak clearly without interruptions.

3. Focus on using "I" statements rather than "you" statements when expressing your emotions. Instead of blaming someone

with statements like, "You always make me feel hurt," say, "I feel hurt when this happens." This strategy makes it easier to avoid sounding accusatory or aggressive.

4. Exercise Active Listening: Active listening is a necessary component of effective emotional expression. Without interfering or passing judgment, let the other person express their point of view. By confirming their sentiments and experiences, you can demonstrate empathy and understanding.

5. Pick Your Words Carefully: Pay attention to the language you employ when expressing your emotions. To express your feelings, use language that is clear and concise. Avoid using aggressive or hurtful language that could make the situation worse or hurt other people.

6. Make Use of Non-Verbal Communication: Emotions can be expressed in large part through non-verbal cues like facial expressions, body language, and tone of voice. Make sure your nonverbal communication reflects the emotions you want to convey by paying attention to it.

7. Express Yourself Through Writing or Art: Verbalizing your emotions isn't always easy. In such circumstances, think about journaling or expressing yourself through the arts, music, or other forms of creativity. These mediums can offer a secure setting for emotional exploration and release.

8. Seek Supportive Listening: If you have trouble expressing your feelings to family members or friends, think about getting help from a therapist, counselor, or support group. These experts can give you advice and give you a nonjudgmental place to express yourself.

9. Practice Emotional Regulation Techniques: Calming techniques like deep breathing, meditation, or physical activity can be beneficial before expressing strong emotions. These techniques

can assist you in controlling your emotions and approaching the conversation with greater composure.

10. Be Honest and Authentic: When expressing your emotions, make an effort to be sincere and true to who you are. Honesty promotes transparent communication that leads to stronger relationships with others.

Healthy Coping Mechanisms

Healthy coping mechanisms are flexible and helpful activities or strategies that people use to successfully handle and get through difficult or stressful circumstances, feelings, or experiences. These coping techniques are meant to foster psychological health, resilience, and emotional well-being. Healthy coping mechanisms are enduring and support overall personal development and wellbeing, in contrast to unhealthy coping mechanisms, which may offer momentary solace but may be harmful or counterproductive over time.

Healthy coping techniques include the following examples:

1. Seeking support: Speaking with dependable friends, family members, or experts to express your feelings and seek counsel or advice.

2. Using self-care techniques, such as exercising, getting enough sleep, meditating, taking breaks, or engaging in hobbies, to promote relaxation, self-nurturing, and self-compassion.

3. Finding healthy outlets for emotion expression and processing, such as journaling, creative expression (art, music, writing), or open communication with a trusted person.

4. Problem-solving is the process of recognizing a problem or stressor and actively seeking solutions, addressing, and resolving it.

5. Establishing healthy boundaries in relationships and commitments, recognizing and stating your needs and limitations, and saying no when necessary are all examples of setting boundaries.

6. Using relaxation techniques: To calm the mind and body and lessen stress, use techniques like deep breathing exercises, progressive muscle relaxation, or guided imagery.

7. Using constructive distractions: Taking part in activities that help you divert your attention from unfavorable ideas or stressors, like taking up a hobby, reading, watching a movie, or spending time in nature.

8. Using positive self-talk: Replacing unfavorable or self-defeating thoughts with ones that are supportive and uplifting, encouraging self-compassion and a more positive outlook.

9. Seeking professional assistance: Speak with a therapist, counselor, or mental health expert for additional support, direction, and coping mechanisms catered to your individual requirements.

10. Taking part in physical activity: Exercising regularly or taking part in physical activities like dancing, yoga, or walking. Endorphins are released, stress hormones are reduced, and mood is generally improved by physical activity.

OVERCOMING OBSTACLES

Managing Obstacles and Failures

1. Recognize Your Emotions: When faced with failures and setbacks, it is normal to feel a variety of emotions, including sadness, disappointment, and frustration. Without passing judgment, permit yourself to acknowledge and experience these feelings. Accept that failures and setbacks are a normal part of life, and that it's normal to feel upset about them.

2. Change Your Perspective: Instead of seeing failures and setbacks as irreversible or insurmountable, change your perspective to see them as chances for development and learning. Recognize that setbacks are only temporary and can teach you important lessons and give you new perspectives that can help you advance.

3. Develop Self-Compassion: Show yourself compassion when you experience setbacks. Give yourself the same consideration and sympathy that you would give to a friend going through a similar circumstance. Remind yourself that failure is a normal part of learning and to refrain from blaming yourself and talking negatively to yourself.

4. Examine and Learn: Take the time to examine what went wrong and determine the elements that caused the failure or setback. This analysis can offer useful information to help prevent similar errors in the future. Instead of dwelling on the negative aspects of the circumstance, be objective and concentrate on the lessons discovered.

5. Modify Your Approach: Make the necessary alterations to your approach or strategy using the knowledge you gained from analyzing the setback. Think about getting opinions from people who have been in comparable circumstances, or speak with a mentor or specialist in the area. Make changes to your current plan or create a new one using the information provided.

6. Have Realistic Expectations: Sometimes failures happen because we had unrealistic expectations or because we put ourselves in a position to fail. Determine whether your expectations and goals were met, and, if not, make any necessary adjustments. Setting attainable goals can boost your confidence and lessen the likelihood of future failure.

7. Seek Support: During trying times, reach out to your network of friends, family, and mentors. Talking about your setbacks and failures with others can offer you emotional support, new viewpoints, and helpful guidance. You can maintain a positive attitude and regain motivation by surrounding yourself with encouraging people.

Overcoming Self-Doubt and Fear

You can use the following steps in your everyday life to get over self-doubt and fear:

1. Recognize and acknowledge your fear and self-doubt: The first step is to become conscious of your fear and self-doubt. Recognize their presence and the fact that they are typical feelings that everyone encounters occasionally.

2. Dispel negative thoughts and beliefs: Negative thoughts and beliefs about ourselves are frequently the root of self-doubt and fear. Start challenging the veracity of these ideas and starting to doubt them. Look for evidence that lends credence to a more upbeat and realistic viewpoint

3. Reframe negative self-talk: Substitute empowering and upbeat statements for negative ones. Use self-affirmations to increase your confidence and serve as a reminder of your talents and past accomplishments.

4. Establish practical objectives and acknowledge small successes: Divide your objectives into manageable, smaller steps. Concentrate on achieving these more manageable objectives,

and enjoy each step along the way. You can overcome self-doubt and increase your confidence by doing this.

5. Act despite your fears: Self-doubt and fear frequently prevent us from acting. Even if it hurts, push yourself to leave your comfort zone and move a little closer to your objectives. Your self-doubt and fear will gradually lessen with each small action you take.

6. Seek out assistance from others. Discuss your difficulties with dependable family members, close friends, or mentors. They can offer support, direction, and a different viewpoint. Be in the company of people who are confident in your abilities and who are supportive of you.

7. Exercise self-compassion: Be kind and understanding to yourself. Keep in mind that everyone makes errors and has setbacks. When difficulties arise, remember to be kind to yourself and that you are doing your best.

8. Visualize success and favorable outcomes: Employ visualization techniques to picture yourself getting past challenges and realizing your objectives. By conjuring an image of success in the mind, visualization can help increase self-assurance and decrease fear

9. If necessary, seek professional assistance: If self-doubt and fear significantly interfere with your daily life or continue despite your efforts, think about consulting a therapist or counselor. They can offer helpful advice, guidance, and support that is catered to your particular requirements.

10. Continue learning and developing: Adopt a growth mindset and see obstacles as chances to advance personally. Learn new things on a regular basis, expand your knowledge, and look for experiences that will force you to step outside of your comfort zone. You can overcome self-doubt and fear by embracing growth and emphasizing progress over perfection

Seeking Professional Help if Needed

It might be beneficial to seek professional assistance if self-doubt and fear continue to negatively impact your day-to-day activities, interpersonal relationships, or general wellbeing. Here are some things to think about:

1. A therapist or counselor can offer direction and support that are suited to your individual needs. They can assist you in developing coping mechanisms, exploring the root causes of your self-doubt and fear, and working to strengthen your confidence and resilience

2. Cognitive-Behavioral Therapy (CBT): CBT is a therapeutic strategy that is frequently used. It focuses on recognizing and changing unfavorable thought patterns and behaviors. A CBT-trained therapist can assist you in confronting self-doubt, reframing unfavorable beliefs, and creating successful coping mechanisms for fear.

3. Support Groups: Becoming a member of a support group can give you a sense of belonging and comprehension. Interacting with people who have gone through similar things can provide insights, inspiration, and helpful advice for overcoming self-doubt and fear.

4. Psychologist or Psychiatrist: In some circumstances, you might need a psychologist or psychiatrist's assistance. They are able to carry out a thorough evaluation, identify any underlying mental health issues, and, if necessary, prescribe the proper medications.

CONCLUSION

- Understanding the importance of thoughts and emotions: Realizing how much our thoughts and feelings affect our general wellbeing and level of happiness.

- Identifying negative thought and emotional patterns that impede personal development and happiness. This is achieved by developing self-awareness.

- Perspective change: Using cognitive retraining and positive thinking strategies, one can challenge unfavorable attitudes and adopt a more upbeat and realistic outlook.

- Developing emotional resilience: Increasing one's capacity to recover from setbacks, creating a network of allies, and engaging in stress management and self-care activities.

- Emotional regulation techniques, such as effective emotion identification and expression, the use of healthy coping mechanisms, and research into journaling and emotional release methods.

- Creating a positive routine, setting realistic goals, and incorporating gratitude and mindfulness exercises into daily life are all examples of how to develop positive habits.

- Fostering healthy connections: Surrounding oneself with uplifting influences, improving communication abilities, and creating conflict-resolution plans.

- Overcoming challenges: Becoming resilient in the face of failures and setbacks, getting past fear and self-doubt, and, if necessary, seeking professional assistance.

- Making a tailored action plan: Evaluating results, establishing objectives, and putting plans into practice while continuously keeping an eye on them and making adjustments as necessary.You can overcome negativity, improve emotional wellbeing, and cultivate a happier life by incorporating these crucial ideas and methods into your daily life. Keep in mind that each person's journey is distinctive, and it calls for dedication, tolerance, and self-compassion.

- Adopting self-awareness and mindfulness: gaining the capacity to objectively observe and comprehend your thoughts, emotions, and reactions. You can stay in the moment and control your emotions by practicing mindfulness.

- Developing self-compassion: Being kind and understanding to yourself when you are dealing with difficult emotions or setbacks. Self-compassion entails being aware of your flaws and showing yourself sympathy and support.

- Leveraging the power of gratitude: Adopting an attitude of gratitude can help you turn your attention to the good things in life. Regularly feeling thankful for what you have can improve your wellbeing in general and combat negativity.

- Prioritizing self-care activities that nourish your mind, body, and soul will help you build resilience. Exercise, a healthy diet, getting enough sleep, and participating in hobbies can all help you be more resilient and emotionally healthy.

- Engaging in effective communication: Improving your communication abilities can promote healthier relationships and reduce miscommunication. Effective communication relies on active listening, empathy, and assertiveness.

Reflecting on your values, interests, and goals can help you find a sense of meaning and purpose in life. A more optimistic outlook can be attained by pursuing meaningful activities and living in accordance with your values.

- Honoring progress and modest victories: Recognizing and applauding even the smallest victories in your battle against negativity. You can be inspired to keep going forward and reinforce positive changes by recognizing your progress.

Keep in mind that these ideas are related and can support one another. Approaching them with an open mind, consistency, and dedication to personal development is key. You can gradually overcome negativity, effectively manage your emotions, and cultivate a more positive and fulfilling life experience by incorporating these practices into your life.

www.ingramcontent.com/pod-product-compliance
Lightning Source LLC
Chambersburg PA
CBHW020330290526
45785CB00007B/2994